CONTENTS

CODE TO COMPLETION

*ENSURING QUALITY
THROUGH THE SOFTWARE
DEVELOPMENT LIFECYCLE*

INTRODUCTION

I n today's fast-paced, technology-driven world, software is the backbone of nearly every industry. From healthcare and finance to retail and education, well-crafted software solutions are crucial to success. Yet, building high-quality software is a complex endeavor, one that requires more than technical expertise—it demands a clear roadmap, a commitment to excellence, and a relentless focus on quality. In "Code to Completion: Ensuring Quality Through the Software Development Lifecycle," I bring 25 years of experience in software development, quality assurance, and project management to explore what it takes to deliver software that meets user needs, withstands real-world challenges, and stands the test of time.

Over the course of my career, I have seen technology transform, development methodologies evolve, and quality standards rise. I have witnessed firsthand the impact of both success and failure in the software lifecycle. Projects with well-defined processes, rigorous quality checks, and clear communication channels have consistently delivered high-value results. Meanwhile, projects that overlooked quality assurance in the early stages often faced costly rework, delayed launches, and unsatisfied users.

This book is intended for developers, project managers, quality assurance professionals, and anyone else involved in software development who wants to enhance their understanding of the Software Development Lifecycle (SDLC) and the role of Quality Assurance (QA). Whether you are just beginning your journey or are an experienced professional looking to deepen your expertise, this guide will provide a practical framework for navigating the SDLC with a strong focus on quality at every stage.

The Software Development Lifecycle, or SDLC, is a roadmap that guides a project from concept to completion. It defines the phases of planning, designing, coding, testing, deployment, and maintenance. Within each of these stages lies the potential for both success and failure, depending on the decisions made, the processes followed, and the emphasis placed on quality. By treating QA as an integral part of each stage rather than an afterthought, teams can save time, reduce costs, and avoid setbacks.

Code to Completion is divided into sections that mirror the SDLC, with each chapter dedicated to a specific phase and the best practices for ensuring quality throughout. We will cover tools and techniques for planning with precision, designing for robustness, coding with efficiency, testing rigorously, and deploying confidently. The book will delve into real-world scenarios and case studies, offering insights into the challenges and solutions encountered in projects large and small.

In software development, quality is more than a goal; it's a journey. It requires proactive measures, strategic planning, and a commitment to improvement. In the pages that follow, we will explore this journey, equipping you with the knowledge and tools to build software that not only works but excels, meeting and exceeding user expectations. Quality is not just the final step of development; it's woven into the fabric of every phase. Join me as we take a deep dive into the SDLC, emphasizing quality every step of the way—from code to completion.

As we move forward in this book, we'll start with the foundational stage of software development: Planning and Requirement Analysis. This phase is where ideas and goals are translated into structured requirements, setting the groundwork for everything that follows. Here, we'll discuss how to gather accurate, detailed requirements, engage stakeholders effectively, and use strategic planning tools to align the development process with project objectives. This section will also introduce the importance of risk assessment and management early on to avoid costly missteps later.

In System Design, we'll shift from "what" the software should do to "how" it will do it. This phase requires careful attention to architecture, data flows, and interface design, as well as ensuring scalability, security, and usability are baked into the blueprint. We'll discuss design principles, modeling techniques, and documentation practices that create a solid foundation for a smooth development process and help facilitate effective collaboration across teams.

Next, in Development/Implementation, we'll explore the process of turning designs into actual code. This chapter will cover coding standards, practices, and methodologies such as Agile and DevOps, which support iterative development and continuous integration. The emphasis will be on writing clean, maintainable code and ensuring that each feature aligns with the project's goals. Here, we'll also introduce techniques for embedding quality checks, like code reviews and pair programming, that reduce errors from the very start.

Following development, Testing takes center stage. This phase is where the value of Quality Assurance is most visible, as it directly impacts the user experience and overall reliability of the software. In this section, we'll delve into testing methodologies, from unit testing and integration testing to system and acceptance testing. We'll also examine automated testing frameworks, continuous testing pipelines, and the balance between automated and manual testing to achieve maximum efficiency and thoroughness. Testing is more than finding bugs; it's about ensuring that the software meets every expectation and requirement set during the planning phase.

Deployment marks the transition from development to production, and it's often where even the best-laid plans can encounter unexpected hurdles. In this chapter, we'll discuss deployment strategies, rollback plans, and monitoring practices to ensure a smooth launch. We'll also cover the importance of post-deployment validation and immediate feedback loops to address any issues that arise swiftly and effectively.

Finally, Maintenance and Support is an

ongoing commitment. This phase keeps software operational and aligned with evolving user needs, system requirements, and technology standards. Here, we'll discuss strategies for managing software updates, patching security vulnerabilities, handling user feedback, and scaling the software as demand grows. Effective maintenance practices are often overlooked, but they are essential to prolonging the life and value of the software.

Each of these SDLC stages will include best practices, real-world examples, and actionable insights for maintaining a high standard of quality. Alongside these technical insights, we'll also touch on the human elements of software development, such as team collaboration, communication, and adaptability. A successful SDLC and QA process is only possible when every team member—from developers and testers to project managers and stakeholders—is aligned in their commitment to quality.

At the end of this journey, you'll have a comprehensive understanding of the Software Development Lifecycle and the key role Quality Assurance plays in every phase. This book isn't just about building functional software; it's about crafting exceptional software that meets the highest standards of quality, security, and performance.

Whether you're working on a small project or a large-scale enterprise application, the principles and practices outlined here are designed to help you succeed. In an industry where technology changes rapidly, quality remains the constant that separates good software from great software. Let's begin this journey together—from code to completion, with quality at the heart of every step.

CHAPTER 1: PLANNING AND REQUIREMENT ANALYSIS

The success of any software project is rooted in the strength of its foundation. Planning and requirement analysis form the first step of the Software Development Lifecycle (SDLC), setting the stage for every decision that will follow. In this chapter, we will cover the essential components of planning and requirement analysis, explore best practices for gathering and documenting requirements, and discuss the importance of aligning these requirements with business goals and user expectations. By the end of this chapter, you will have a blueprint for effectively initiating a project with clarity, precision, and purpose.

1.1 Importance of the Planning Phase

The planning phase defines the scope, objectives, and overall strategy of the project. Often, this phase is the difference between projects that succeed and those that fail. Effective planning reduces uncertainties, minimizes risks, and aligns teams on the project's vision. Failing to devote adequate time to planning often results in costly rework, scope creep, missed deadlines, and dissatisfaction among stakeholders.

This phase isn't just about making initial decisions —it's about setting a clear roadmap for the project. A strong plan answers the following questions:

What are we building?

Why is it important?

Who will use it, and how?

What risks and constraints should we consider?

These answers will become the guideposts that lead the project from concept to completion.

1.2 Requirement Gathering: Translating Ideas into Concrete Goals

Requirement gathering is one of the most critical parts of the planning phase. During this process, teams work closely with stakeholders—

users, business leaders, and other key parties—
to understand what the software must achieve.
The goal is to translate broad ideas into specific,
actionable requirements that can guide the entire
development process.

Techniques for Requirement Gathering

Interviews: Conducting one-on-one or group
interviews with stakeholders to gain insights into
their needs and expectations.

Workshops: Engaging stakeholders in workshops
where brainstorming, problem-solving, and
discussions occur. Workshops can be especially
helpful for gaining diverse perspectives.

Surveys and Questionnaires: Using structured
surveys can provide a quick way to gather input
from a large group of users or stakeholders.

Observation: Watching how users interact with
current systems or processes provides insights that
might not emerge through interviews or surveys
alone.

Prototyping: Creating mockups or low-fidelity
prototypes to gather feedback on the user

experience and functionality before development begins.

Types of Requirements

Requirements generally fall into two main categories:

Functional Requirements: Define what the system should do. For example, "The system must allow users to register and log in with their email."

Non-Functional Requirements: Define how the system should perform. This includes performance, security, usability, and scalability requirements. For instance, "The system should handle up to 10,000 concurrent users without performance degradation."

Each requirement should be documented clearly and comprehensively to prevent ambiguity.

1.3 Documenting Requirements: Creating a Clear, Usable Blueprint

Once requirements are gathered, they must be documented in a way that's accessible and understandable for all project members. Good documentation ensures that developers, testers, and stakeholders have a shared understanding of what the project will deliver.

Common Documentation Formats

Software Requirement Specification (SRS): An SRS document includes detailed descriptions of functional and non-functional requirements, system interactions, constraints, and more. This is typically the primary document guiding development.

User Stories: Popular in Agile methodologies, user stories are brief descriptions of features from the end-user's perspective, such as, "As a user, I want to reset my password so I can regain access to my account."

Use Cases: Use cases outline the interactions between users and the system, specifying the steps needed to achieve particular goals.

Wireframes and Prototypes: Visual representations of the interface and user flows, which help stakeholders envision the end product and provide feedback early in the design phase.

Key Principles for Documentation

Clarity: Avoid technical jargon or vague terms. Requirements should be understandable to all stakeholders.

Specificity: Each requirement should be precise and measurable to avoid ambiguity.

Prioritization: Not all requirements are equal. Prioritizing requirements based on business value and feasibility ensures that essential features are completed first.

1.4 Aligning Requirements with Business Objectives

Requirement analysis isn't just about gathering functional specifications—it's about ensuring that every requirement aligns with business objectives. This alignment is crucial because even a perfectly executed project may fall short if it doesn't meet the intended business goals.

During planning, ask questions such as:

How does this requirement contribute to our overall business objectives?

Will this feature add value to the user experience?

Are there any requirements that could be deprioritized or removed to better align with the project's mission?

Engaging business leaders, stakeholders, and users in this process helps ensure that resources are spent on the most valuable features and functionalities.

1.5 Risk Analysis: Identifying and Mitigating Potential Roadblocks

Every project has risks, whether they're technical, financial, or timeline-related. The planning phase is the best time to identify potential risks and develop mitigation strategies.

Types of Risks

Technical Risks: Challenges with technologies, integrations, or data handling.

Operational Risks: Potential issues with team coordination, resource availability, or communication.

Market Risks: Risks that stem from changing user expectations, competitor activities, or external market forces.

Risk Mitigation Techniques

Risk Assessment Matrix: Create a risk matrix to prioritize risks based on their likelihood and potential impact.

Contingency Plans: Develop contingency plans for high-priority risks to ensure the team is prepared to respond if these issues arise.

Regular Risk Reviews: Periodically review risks throughout the SDLC to address new challenges as they emerge.

1.6 Key Takeaways and Best Practices

Planning and requirement analysis form the backbone of the SDLC. By investing time and effort in this phase, teams can reduce risks, ensure alignment with business objectives, and set clear, actionable requirements that guide the project from start to finish. Here are the key takeaways from this chapter:

Involve Stakeholders: Early and continuous involvement of stakeholders ensures that requirements are accurate and aligned with expectations.

Use Multiple Techniques: Combining interviews, workshops, surveys, and prototypes offers a well-rounded understanding of requirements.

Prioritize Requirements: Focus on the most impactful requirements to deliver the highest business value.

Document Thoroughly: Good documentation ensures that all project members share a common understanding of requirements and goals.

Prepare for Risks: Identify potential risks early and develop mitigation strategies to protect the project from unexpected challenges.

With a solid foundation built through effective planning and thorough requirement analysis, the project can move into the next phase with confidence. In the following chapter, we'll explore System Design, where we translate these requirements into a technical blueprint that will guide development.

CHAPTER 2:
SYSTEM DESIGN

With the project's requirements defined, documented, and aligned with business objectives, the next step in the Software Development Lifecycle (SDLC) is System Design. This phase translates the "what" of the requirements phase into the "how"—how the software will function, how components will interact, and how the system will meet performance and security standards. In this chapter, we'll explore key design principles, methodologies, and tools to create a robust, scalable, and user-centered software architecture.

2.1 The Goals of System Design

System design is essential for creating a cohesive structure that can accommodate current requirements and adapt to future needs. A well-designed system is more maintainable, scalable, and resilient to changes, which translates into long-term efficiency and reduced costs.

The goals of system design include:

Defining Architecture: Establishing a high-level structure for the software, including system components, modules, and data flows.

Ensuring Scalability: Designing the system to handle increased loads and growing user demands.

Enhancing Security: Incorporating measures to protect user data, ensure data privacy, and defend against cyber threats.

Optimizing Performance: Structuring the system for speed and responsiveness, even under peak usage.

Supporting Maintainability: Ensuring the design facilitates easy updates, bug fixes, and new feature integrations.

By the end of the design phase, there should be a clear and comprehensive blueprint that guides the development team in bringing the software to life.

2.2 Design Methodologies

Several design methodologies can help guide the

process, each with its own strengths and ideal use cases. Here are a few of the most common approaches:

2.2.1 Object-Oriented Design (OOD)

Object-oriented design focuses on structuring software around objects, which are instances of classes that represent entities with both data and behaviors. This approach allows for modular, reusable code, which can improve maintainability and scalability.

Key principles of OOD include:

Encapsulation: Bundling data and functions that operate on that data within a single unit, or object.

Inheritance: Allowing new objects to inherit properties and methods from existing ones, promoting code reuse.

Polymorphism: Enabling objects to be treated as instances of their parent class, allowing for more flexible code.

Abstraction: Hiding complex implementation details behind simpler interfaces, making the software easier to use and extend.

2.2.2 Service-Oriented Architecture (SOA)

Service-oriented architecture organizes software as a collection of services, where each service is a self-contained unit with a specific function. SOA is ideal for systems with complex, distributed operations, as it allows different services to communicate over a network.

Advantages of SOA include:

Interoperability: Services can be reused across different applications or platforms.

Scalability: Services can be scaled independently, enabling better resource management.

Flexibility: Services can be modified or replaced with minimal impact on other parts of the system.

2.2.3 Microservices Architecture

Microservices architecture is a specific form of SOA that focuses on breaking down a system into small, independently deployable services. Each microservice is designed to perform a specific business function and can be developed, tested, and deployed separately.

Benefits of microservices include:

Agility: Teams can develop and deploy services

independently, which speeds up delivery.

Resilience: If one service fails, it doesn't necessarily impact the entire system.

Improved Scaling: Each microservice can be scaled independently, optimizing resources based on demand.

2.2.4 Model-View-Controller (MVC)

MVC is a design pattern used primarily in web development. It separates the application into three components:

Model: Manages the data and business logic.

View: Handles the user interface and presentation.

Controller: Acts as an intermediary, processing user input and updating the model or view as needed.

MVC promotes separation of concerns, making code easier to manage, test, and modify.

2.3 Defining the System Architecture

Once a design methodology has been chosen, the next step is to define the system's architecture. The architecture specifies how different components interact, including how data flows between them, how users interact with the system, and how various functionalities are organized.

Common Architectural Patterns

Layered (n-Tier) Architecture: This approach divides the system into layers, each responsible for a specific part of the process, such as the presentation layer, business logic layer, and data access layer.

Client-Server Architecture: The system is divided into clients, which request services, and a server, which provides them. This model is commonly used in applications requiring central data management, such as web applications.

Event-Driven Architecture: Components react to events (e.g., changes in data) and respond accordingly. This architecture is highly responsive and often used in real-time applications like chat services or IoT.

Microkernel Architecture: Consists of a core system (the microkernel) with plug-ins for additional features. This architecture is commonly used in applications that require frequent updates or customization.

Selecting the Right Architecture

Choosing the right architecture depends on project requirements, scalability needs, and the level of complexity. For example:

Layered architecture is ideal for enterprise applications that need modular separation.

Microservices work well for large, complex systems that require high scalability and independent deployments.

Event-driven suits applications needing quick, real-time responses.

2.4 Data Flow and Storage Design

An essential part of system design is determining how data will flow through the system and how it will be stored. This includes defining databases, data schemas, and storage solutions that align with system requirements.

Key Considerations for Data Design

Data Integrity: Ensuring data accuracy and consistency across the system.

Performance: Optimizing data retrieval and storage to support fast response times.

Scalability: Designing databases that can handle increasing amounts of data without performance loss.

Security: Implementing encryption and access controls to protect sensitive data.

Database Options

Relational Databases (SQL): Ideal for structured data with defined relationships. Examples include MySQL, PostgreSQL, and Oracle.

NoSQL Databases: Suitable for unstructured or semi-structured data, often used for scalable, distributed applications. Examples include MongoDB, Cassandra, and CouchDB.

Data Lakes and Warehouses: Used for large-scale data storage and analytics, particularly in systems with big data needs.

2.5 Security and Compliance

Security is a non-negotiable part of system design, especially in applications that handle sensitive data. By incorporating security measures into the design phase, developers can minimize vulnerabilities and protect user data from cyber threats.

Security Principles

Data Encryption: Encrypting sensitive data, both in transit and at rest, to prevent unauthorized access.

Authentication and Authorization: Implementing strong user authentication (e.g., multi-factor authentication) and defining user roles with appropriate access levels.

Regular Security Audits: Planning for ongoing vulnerability assessments and penetration testing to identify and fix security issues.

Compliance Considerations

For software that handles personal or financial data, compliance with regulations such as GDPR, HIPAA, or CCPA is essential. Understanding these requirements early in the design phase helps ensure the system aligns with legal standards.

2.6 Creating Design Documentation

Once the architecture and design decisions are made, it's crucial to document them clearly. Design documentation provides a reference for developers, testers, and other stakeholders, ensuring everyone has a shared understanding of the system's structure and objectives.

Essential Components of Design Documentation

System Architecture Diagram: A visual representation of components and their interactions.

Data Flow Diagrams: Diagrams showing how data moves through the system.

API Specifications: Descriptions of any application programming interfaces, including endpoints, methods, and expected inputs/outputs.

Security Protocols: A summary of the security measures and compliance standards the system follows.

2.7 Key Takeaways and Best Practices

System design is a critical phase in the SDLC, as it sets the technical foundation for development. Here are some best practices to keep in mind:

Choose the Right Architecture: Match the architecture to project requirements, scalability needs, and complexity.

Prioritize Security and Compliance: Integrate security and regulatory requirements into the design from the beginning.

Document Thoroughly: Clear, comprehensive documentation ensures that developers and stakeholders have a shared understanding of the design.

Focus on Scalability: Design with future growth in mind, particularly in areas like data storage and system performance.

With a solid design in place, the development team is equipped to move forward confidently. In the next chapter, we will cover Development and Implementation, exploring how to translate this design into functional, reliable code.

CHAPTER 3:
DEVELOPMENT AND
IMPLEMENTATION

With a comprehensive system design in place, we now move into the Development and Implementation phase. This phase is where the vision becomes reality—the architecture, design specifications, and requirements established in the previous stages are transformed into actual code. Development is one of the most dynamic stages of the Software Development Lifecycle (SDLC), involving collaboration, testing, and iteration to bring the product to life.

In this chapter, we'll cover the coding process, best practices for writing maintainable and scalable code, methodologies that streamline development, and techniques for ensuring quality throughout implementation. By the end of this chapter, you'll understand how to develop software that aligns with the requirements, design, and quality standards established in the earlier phases.

3.1 Development Methodologies

Different development methodologies provide various frameworks and approaches to guide the coding process. The right methodology can enhance team productivity, streamline communication, and ensure that development aligns closely with the project's goals. Here are some commonly used methodologies:

3.1.1 Agile Development

Agile is a flexible, iterative approach to software development that emphasizes collaboration, customer feedback, and rapid delivery. In Agile, development is broken into short cycles called "sprints," typically lasting two to four weeks. After each sprint, a usable piece of the software is delivered, allowing stakeholders to provide feedback and adjustments to be made quickly.

Key principles of Agile include:

Customer Collaboration: Regularly involving

stakeholders to refine requirements and adapt to changing needs.

Iterative Delivery: Releasing software incrementally, so that improvements and new features are added over time.

Adaptability: Embracing change, even late in development, to better meet user needs.

3.1.2 DevOps

DevOps combines development and operations to streamline the entire software delivery process, from coding to deployment. This methodology emphasizes collaboration between development, QA, and operations teams, often incorporating automation to improve efficiency and reduce errors.

Benefits of DevOps include:

Continuous Integration and Continuous Delivery (CI/CD): Automating testing and deployment to catch issues early and speed up delivery.

Enhanced Collaboration: Bridging the gap between development and operations for smoother deployments.

Improved Reliability: Monitoring and feedback loops allow for rapid identification and resolution of issues.

3.1.3 Waterfall

Waterfall is a more traditional, sequential approach to development. Each phase must be completed before the next begins. While less flexible than Agile, Waterfall can be suitable for projects with well-defined requirements and a low likelihood of significant changes.

Advantages of Waterfall include:

Clear Structure: Each phase has a distinct beginning and end, making it easier to manage progress.

Comprehensive Documentation: Detailed documentation ensures that requirements are well understood before coding begins.

3.2 Writing High-Quality Code

Good code is readable, efficient, and easy to maintain. Following coding best practices improves code quality, making it easier for other developers to understand and modify the software in the future. Here are some key principles:

3.2.1 Code Readability

Readable code is essential for collaboration and future maintenance. Code should be organized and written in a way that's easy to follow, even by developers who didn't originally write it.

Best practices for readability include:

Consistent Naming Conventions: Use meaningful, descriptive names for variables, functions, and classes.

Code Comments and Documentation: Use comments to explain complex logic and document each function's purpose, inputs, and outputs.

Logical Structure: Use clear indentation, spacing, and line breaks to improve readability.

3.2.2 Modularity and Reusability

Modular code is broken down into separate functions or classes, each handling a specific task. This approach allows code to be reused, making it easier to test, debug, and maintain.

Ways to improve modularity:

Function Decomposition: Break complex functions into smaller, simpler ones, each handling a specific part of the logic.

Avoid Hardcoding Values: Use constants or configuration files to store values that may need to change, like API keys or file paths.

3.2.3 Error Handling

Good error handling ensures that the system can handle unexpected inputs or failures gracefully, improving reliability and user experience.

Error handling best practices:

Use Try-Catch Blocks: Capture exceptions to prevent system crashes and provide useful error messages.

Log Errors: Store error logs for debugging, making it easier to identify and fix issues.

Validate User Inputs: Ensure inputs are valid before processing to prevent errors or security vulnerabilities.

3.3 Continuous Integration and Continuous Delivery (CI/CD)

CI/CD is a DevOps practice that automates code integration, testing, and delivery. It enables developers to detect errors early and release new code faster and more reliably.

Continuous Integration (CI)

Continuous Integration involves merging code from

different developers frequently, often several times a day. Each merge triggers automated tests to detect any issues early.

Benefits of CI:

Early Detection of Errors: By integrating code frequently, issues are identified and resolved early in development.

Improved Collaboration: Frequent integrations encourage collaboration and reduce code conflicts.

Automated Testing: Tests are automatically run on each merge, saving time and effort.

Continuous Delivery (CD)

Continuous Delivery automates the process of delivering code changes to production. While CI tests for functionality, CD ensures that the system is always ready for deployment.

Benefits of CD:

Faster Releases: Automating the release process reduces deployment time and allows for rapid updates.

Reduced Risk: Small, frequent releases minimize the

risk of major issues during deployment.

Improved Quality: With automated tests and feedback loops, developers can ensure a high-quality product.

3.4 Unit Testing and Code Reviews

Testing and code reviews are crucial for catching bugs and ensuring code quality before it goes live. These practices not only identify errors but also improve code structure and readability.

Unit Testing

Unit tests check individual components or functions to ensure they work as expected. A robust set of unit tests can catch issues early and prevent them from affecting the rest of the system.

Best practices for unit testing:

Test Edge Cases: Test not only typical inputs but also unusual or extreme cases.

Mock Dependencies: Use mock objects to isolate the component being tested, reducing dependencies.

Automate Testing: Automated tests can be run frequently, catching issues earlier in the development process.

Code Reviews

Code reviews involve having one or more developers review another's code for quality, readability, and adherence to best practices. Reviews are a powerful tool for knowledge sharing, collaboration, and continuous improvement.

Best practices for code reviews:

Set Clear Guidelines: Establish coding standards and expectations to ensure consistency.

Encourage Constructive Feedback: Reviews should be positive, focusing on learning and improvement.

Use Review Tools: Platforms like GitHub or Bitbucket provide tools for tracking comments and changes, making reviews more efficient.

3.5 Tracking and Managing Progress

Development progress should be tracked to ensure the project stays on schedule and within scope. Progress tracking tools provide visibility, helping teams identify and address delays early.

Common tracking practices:

Daily Stand-ups: Short meetings where each team

member provides an update on their progress, highlighting any blockers.

Task Management Tools: Tools like Jira, Asana, or Trello help break down tasks and track progress.

Burndown Charts: Used in Agile to visually track progress and ensure the team is on pace to complete tasks within the sprint.

3.6 Documentation and Knowledge Sharing

Documentation is often overlooked during development but is crucial for long-term success. By documenting code, processes, and decisions, teams make it easier for future developers to understand and maintain the software.

Key documentation types:

API Documentation: Clearly document each API endpoint, including parameters, responses, and error codes.

Technical Documentation: Record system architecture, database schemas, and key algorithms.

User Documentation: Provide instructions for users, including installation guides, troubleshooting tips, and FAQs.

Knowledge sharing through documentation, team

meetings, and mentorship ensures that every team member is informed and prepared to contribute effectively.

3.7 Key Takeaways and Best Practices

The Development and Implementation phase transforms ideas into reality, with code being the primary output. Here are the key takeaways:

Choose the Right Development Methodology: Select the methodology that best aligns with project needs, whether it's Agile, DevOps, or Waterfall.

Write Clean, Readable Code: Prioritize readability, modularity, and proper error handling.

Implement CI/CD: Use CI/CD pipelines to automate testing and deployment, enhancing efficiency and reducing errors.

Conduct Code Reviews and Testing: Frequent code reviews and unit testing help ensure quality at every step.

Track Progress and Document Thoroughly: Track development progress and document code and processes for easier maintenance and future development.

With development complete, the software is ready to move into the Testing phase, where it will undergo rigorous quality checks to ensure it meets the highest standards. In the next chapter, we'll explore the role of Quality Assurance, the different types of testing, and how to catch issues before the software reaches end users.

CHAPTER 4: TESTING AND QUALITY ASSURANCE

After the code has been written, the next essential phase in the Software Development Lifecycle (SDLC) is Testing and Quality Assurance (QA). This phase ensures that the software meets the requirements specified in the planning phase, functions as intended, and provides a reliable, secure, and enjoyable user experience. Testing isn't just about finding bugs; it's about verifying that every part of the software performs optimally under various conditions, meets quality standards, and satisfies the end-user requirements.

In this chapter, we'll cover the role of QA in the SDLC, the different types of testing, how to implement an effective testing strategy, and the tools and techniques that streamline the QA process.

By the end of this chapter, you'll understand how to approach testing as a proactive, continuous process that contributes to the software's quality and reliability.

4.1 The Role of Quality Assurance in the SDLC

Quality Assurance is a systematic process that ensures the software meets specific requirements and performs reliably. QA is not just a single stage but an ongoing focus throughout the SDLC, from initial planning to final deployment. Effective QA reduces the likelihood of costly bugs in production, enhances user satisfaction, and ensures that the software can withstand real-world usage.

The goals of QA include:

Defining Standards: Establishing quality benchmarks that the software must meet.

Ensuring Functionality: Verifying that each component and feature works as specified.

Enhancing Usability: Ensuring the software is intuitive and easy to use.

Improving Performance: Ensuring the system performs optimally under different conditions.

Strengthening Security: Protecting the system

against vulnerabilities and unauthorized access.

4.2 Types of Testing

There are various types of testing, each designed to address different aspects of software quality. A robust testing strategy combines multiple types of tests to ensure comprehensive coverage and quality assurance.

4.2.1 Unit Testing

Unit testing focuses on individual components or functions of the software, ensuring each unit works as expected. It's often the first level of testing performed after coding.

Purpose: Identify issues in specific functions or methods early.

Tools: JUnit, NUnit, Mocha, and Jest

Best Practices: Test edge cases, isolate dependencies with mocks, and ensure tests are fast and automated.

4.2.2 Integration Testing

Integration testing examines how different components work together. This is especially important in complex systems with multiple modules or services.

Purpose: Ensure that individual modules interact correctly and data flows smoothly between them.

Tools: Postman, Cypress and Selenium.

Best Practices: Test interfaces between modules, simulate real data flows, and prioritize interactions with high impact on functionality.

4.2.3 System Testing

System testing evaluates the entire application as a whole. It verifies that all components work together to meet the specified requirements.

Purpose: Validate end-to-end functionality and performance in an environment similar to production.

Tools: TestRail, Selenium, and Puppeteer.

Best Practices: Conduct tests in a controlled environment, simulate typical user interactions, and cover all critical paths.

4.2.4 User Acceptance Testing (UAT)

User Acceptance Testing is the final phase before deployment, where actual users test the software to ensure it meets their needs and expectations.

Purpose: Validate that the software is ready for production from a user perspective.

Tools: Zephyr, TestRail, and Xray.

Best Practices: Involve real users, create realistic scenarios, and collect detailed feedback to address usability issues.

4.2.5 Performance Testing

Performance testing assesses the software's speed, scalability, and stability under different loads.

Purpose: Ensure the software can handle expected and peak loads without degrading performance.

Types: Load testing, stress testing, and endurance testing.

Tools: JMeter, LoadRunner, and Octoperf

Best Practices: Test with realistic workloads, monitor resource usage, and identify bottlenecks.

4.2.6 Security Testing

Security testing identifies vulnerabilities that could be exploited by attackers. This includes testing for data protection, access control, and resilience against attacks.

Purpose: Protect user data and prevent unauthorized access.

Types: Penetration testing, vulnerability scanning, and ethical hacking.

Tools: OWASP ZAP, Burp Suite, and Nessus.

Best Practices: Conduct tests regularly, simulate real attack vectors, and prioritize critical vulnerabilities.

4.3 Automated Testing vs. Manual Testing

A balanced testing strategy typically includes both automated and manual testing. Each has its strengths and best use cases.

Automated Testing

Automated testing uses scripts to execute tests, which makes it ideal for repetitive tasks, regression testing, and large projects. Automated tests run faster, can be executed frequently, and reduce the chances of human error.

Best for: Unit, integration, and performance testing, where repetitive tasks are common.

Benefits: Speed, consistency, and scalability.

Challenges: Initial setup time and maintenance can

be high, especially for complex test cases.

Manual Testing

Manual testing involves testers executing tests without automation. This approach is ideal for exploratory testing, UAT, and cases where human judgment is needed, such as evaluating usability or user experience.

Best for: User Acceptance Testing, exploratory testing, and tests requiring human judgment.

Benefits: Flexibility, intuitive insights, and better for ad hoc or non-repetitive tasks.

Challenges: Time-consuming, may not be scalable for large projects.

4.4 Implementing an Effective Testing Strategy

Creating a comprehensive testing strategy ensures that all aspects of the software are tested thoroughly, efficiently, and cost-effectively. An effective strategy should consider the software's complexity, risk areas, and project timeline.

Steps to Implement a Testing Strategy

Define Objectives: Determine what you want to achieve with testing—whether it's functional validation, performance verification, or user satisfaction.

Prioritize Tests: Focus on high-risk areas, critical paths, and core functionalities. Not all tests require the same depth or frequency.

Combine Testing Types: Use a mix of unit, integration, system, and performance tests to cover all aspects of the software.

Automate When Feasible: Automate tests that are repetitive, time-consuming, or frequently run, especially regression tests.

Incorporate QA Early: Integrate testing and quality assurance from the beginning to catch issues before they become more complex and costly.

Review and Iterate: Regularly review test results and adapt the strategy to address emerging issues or changes in project scope.

4.5 Tools for Quality Assurance and Testing

Testing tools help teams streamline the QA process, execute tests efficiently, and analyze results. Here are some popular tools:

Test Management Tools: Jira, TestRail, and Xray help manage test cases, track defects, and report on testing progress.

Automated Testing Tools: Selenium, JUnit, and Appium enable automated tests for web and mobile applications.

Performance Testing Tools: JMeter and LoadRunner provide load testing to assess performance under stress.

Security Testing Tools: OWASP ZAP and Burp Suite help identify security vulnerabilities and simulate attacks.

4.6 Key Metrics for QA and Testing

To assess the effectiveness of your QA efforts, track key metrics that provide insights into software quality and testing efficiency.

Defect Density: Measures the number of defects relative to the size of the codebase, indicating the quality of the code.

Test Coverage: Reflects the percentage of code or functionality covered by tests, showing how much of the system has been validated.

Pass/Fail Rate: The percentage of tests that pass or fail, providing insights into current software stability.

Mean Time to Detect (MTTD): The average time to detect a defect, indicating how quickly issues are identified.

Mean Time to Repair (MTTR): The average time to resolve issues, showing the responsiveness of the QA and development teams.

4.7 Key Takeaways and Best Practices

Testing and Quality Assurance are essential for ensuring that software is reliable, secure, and meets user expectations. Here are the key takeaways:

Diversify Testing Types: Use a mix of testing types to cover functionality, performance, security, and usability.

Balance Automation and Manual Testing: Automate repetitive tasks and regression tests, but rely on manual testing for usability and exploratory testing.

Track QA Metrics: Use metrics like defect density and test coverage to monitor and improve QA effectiveness.

Integrate QA Early and Continuously: Shift-left testing—integrating QA early—reduces issues and aligns development with quality standards.

Continuously Improve: Regularly review test cases, tools, and processes to adapt to changes in requirements, technology, and user expectations.

With thorough testing and quality assurance, the software is ready for the next step: deployment. In the following chapter, we'll discuss the deployment process, strategies for successful releases, and techniques for ensuring a smooth transition from development to production.

CHAPTER 5: DEPLOYMENT AND RELEASE MANAGEMENT

With testing complete and quality assured, the software is ready for deployment. Deployment is the process of moving the software from a development environment into a production environment, where it will be accessible to end users. This stage is crucial—it's where all the work done in previous stages comes together, and even minor mistakes can impact the software's success. A successful deployment ensures that users experience a stable, functional product from day one.

In this chapter, we'll explore the deployment process, strategies for minimizing risk, common deployment models, and best practices for managing a successful release. By the end of this chapter, you'll understand how to approach deployment as a strategic, organized process that ensures the software is launched smoothly and effectively.

5.1 Understanding the Deployment Process

Deployment isn't just a one-time event; it's a series of coordinated steps designed to ensure the software is correctly installed, configured, and running smoothly. Depending on the project's scale, deployment can range from simple to complex and often involves multiple environments, such as staging and production.

Key Stages of Deployment

Preparation: Finalizing the build, verifying configurations, and preparing deployment scripts or tools.

Staging: Deploying the software to a staging environment that mimics production. This is a final opportunity to catch any last-minute issues.

Production Deployment: Moving the software to the live environment and performing final checks.

Validation and Monitoring: Ensuring the software

is functioning correctly and monitoring for any unexpected issues.

5.2 Deployment Models

Choosing the right deployment model depends on factors such as the complexity of the system, expected downtime, and the number of users affected. Here are some common deployment models:

5.2.1 Big Bang Deployment

Big Bang Deployment is a straightforward approach where the entire system is released at once. It's often used for small projects or updates with minimal dependencies.

Advantages: Simple and fast.

Disadvantages: Risky, as any issues affect the entire system and can disrupt all users.

5.2.2 Phased (or Incremental) Deployment

In phased deployment, the software is released in stages, with parts of the system or subsets of users getting access first. This approach allows the team to monitor each phase for issues before proceeding.

Advantages: Reduces risk by allowing incremental

rollout.

Disadvantages: Slower release and requires careful coordination.

5.2.3 Blue-Green Deployment

Blue-Green Deployment involves two identical environments: "blue" and "green." The new version is deployed to the "blue" environment while the "green" environment remains live. Once the new version is validated, traffic is switched from "green" to "blue."

Advantages: Minimal downtime, easy rollback if issues arise.

Disadvantages: Requires double infrastructure, which can be costly.

5.2.4 Rolling Deployment

Rolling Deployment gradually updates parts of the system or groups of users, replacing instances incrementally. This approach is commonly used in distributed or microservices architectures.

Advantages: Allows continuous delivery with minimal disruption.

Disadvantages: Can complicate tracking and managing multiple versions.

5.2.5 Canary Deployment

In a canary deployment, the new version is rolled out to a small, controlled group of users first. Based on their feedback, the software is then gradually released to a larger audience.

Advantages: Provides early feedback, reduces risk.

Disadvantages: Requires monitoring and the ability to manage different versions.

5.3 Deployment Automation

Automating the deployment process reduces the risk of human error, speeds up the release, and makes it easier to deploy frequently and consistently. Automation is essential for CI/CD pipelines and DevOps practices, enabling teams to deploy quickly and with confidence.

Benefits of Deployment Automation

Consistency: Reduces variability and ensures the same steps are followed for each deployment.

Speed: Accelerates deployment time, allowing for more frequent updates.

Reliability: Minimizes human error and provides a repeatable process.

Tools for Deployment Automation

Some popular deployment automation tools include:

Jenkins: A CI/CD tool that integrates with various environments and automates testing and deployment.

Docker: Provides containerization, allowing applications to run consistently across different environments.

Kubernetes: Manages containerized applications, automating deployment, scaling, and operations.

Ansible, Chef, and Puppet: Configuration management tools that automate the setup, configuration, and management of servers and environments.

5.4 Best Practices for Deployment

Deploying software can be complex and risky. Following best practices helps reduce downtime, minimize errors, and ensure a smooth user experience.

5.4.1 Ensure Pre-Deployment Validation

Before deploying to production, verify that all tests have passed, configurations are correct, and the deployment scripts have been tested in staging. This final review helps avoid last-minute surprises.

5.4.2 Use Feature Toggles

Feature toggles, or flags, allow teams to enable or disable specific features in production without redeploying the code. This is especially useful for releasing partially completed features or performing A/B testing.

5.4.3 Establish a Rollback Plan

Even with thorough testing, issues can still arise during deployment. Having a rollback plan allows the team to revert to a stable version if problems occur, minimizing downtime and user impact.

5.4.4 Communicate with Stakeholders

Inform stakeholders, including end users, about the deployment schedule, potential downtime, and any expected changes. Clear communication reduces frustration and sets expectations for when the software will be available.

5.4.5 Monitor the Deployment

During and after deployment, monitor the system's performance, error rates, and user feedback.

Monitoring tools like New Relic, Datadog, and Splunk provide real-time insights into system health, helping teams detect and resolve issues quickly.

5.5 Post-Deployment Validation and Monitoring

After deployment, validating that the software is running correctly and monitoring for issues are critical steps. These activities ensure that the deployment was successful and that any post-release issues are quickly identified and addressed.

Key Post-Deployment Checks

Functionality: Ensure that all core features are working as expected.

Performance: Check load times, response rates, and resource usage to confirm that the software meets performance standards.

Security: Verify that security settings are intact, access controls are enforced, and no vulnerabilities have been introduced.

User Feedback: Collect feedback from early users to identify potential usability issues or unexpected behaviors.

Continuous Monitoring

Continuous monitoring provides ongoing insights into the software's performance and user behavior. It helps the team proactively address issues, optimize performance, and improve the software based on real-world usage.

Key aspects of continuous monitoring include:

Error Tracking: Automatically log and categorize errors to identify trends and recurring issues.

Performance Metrics: Monitor response times, throughput, and resource utilization.

User Analytics: Track user interactions to understand usage patterns and identify areas for improvement.

5.6 Key Takeaways and Best Practices

Deployment is a critical phase that brings the software to end users. Following a structured approach reduces risks, minimizes downtime, and ensures a positive user experience. Here are the key takeaways:

Choose the Right Deployment Model: Select a deployment model that aligns with the project's complexity, user impact, and infrastructure.

Automate Deployment: Deployment automation

reduces errors, speeds up releases, and enables frequent deployments.

Validate Pre-Deployment: Ensure all tests have passed and configurations are correct before deploying to production.

Have a Rollback Plan: Prepare a rollback plan to revert to a stable version in case of unexpected issues.

Monitor Post-Deployment: Validate functionality, monitor performance, and gather user feedback to ensure a successful release.

With deployment complete, the software has reached production, but the journey doesn't end here. The final phase of the SDLC is Maintenance and Support, where the focus shifts to ensuring the software remains functional, secure, and up-to-date. In the next chapter, we'll cover how to manage maintenance effectively, including bug fixes, updates, and responding to user feedback.

CHAPTER 6:
MAINTENANCE
AND SUPPORT

Once software is deployed to production, it enters the Maintenance and Support phase. This phase is essential for ensuring the software remains operational, secure, and relevant to user needs over time. Maintenance involves monitoring the system, fixing bugs, addressing security vulnerabilities, and implementing enhancements or new features as requirements evolve. Effective maintenance sustains user satisfaction, extends the software's lifespan, and enhances its value to the organization.

In this chapter, we'll explore the different types of maintenance, best practices for managing software updates, and how to address issues promptly and efficiently. By the end of this chapter, you'll have a roadmap for providing long-term support that keeps the software running smoothly and adapts to changing needs.

6.1 Types of Software Maintenance

Software maintenance can be divided into several categories, each addressing different aspects of support and improvement. Understanding these categories helps prioritize maintenance activities based on urgency, impact, and strategic value.

6.1.1 Corrective Maintenance

Corrective maintenance involves identifying and fixing bugs or defects in the software. This type of maintenance is often urgent, as it addresses issues that affect the software's functionality or user experience.

Purpose: Restore functionality by correcting errors or bugs discovered post-deployment.

Best Practices: Use error logs and monitoring tools to identify and prioritize bugs, and implement a structured process for testing fixes before deployment.

6.1.2 Adaptive Maintenance

Adaptive maintenance involves modifying the

software to ensure compatibility with evolving environments, such as operating system updates, hardware changes, or new regulatory requirements.

Purpose: Ensure the software remains compatible and compliant as external factors change.

Best Practices: Track dependencies, regularly review external changes that may impact compatibility, and perform regression testing to ensure that updates don't introduce new issues.

6.1.3 Perfective Maintenance

Perfective maintenance focuses on enhancing the software's performance, usability, or features based on user feedback or new business requirements. It's often driven by a desire to improve user satisfaction and keep the software relevant.

Purpose: Improve the software's effectiveness, usability, or performance by adding new features or refining existing ones.

Best Practices: Gather user feedback, prioritize enhancements based on value, and design improvements to be modular and scalable.

6.1.4 Preventive Maintenance

Preventive maintenance is proactive, aiming to prevent future issues by identifying potential vulnerabilities or inefficiencies. This type of maintenance focuses on optimizing the codebase and system to improve reliability and reduce the risk of future failures.

Purpose: Reduce the likelihood of issues by addressing potential weaknesses or inefficiencies.

Best Practices: Conduct regular code reviews, refactor code to improve maintainability, and update libraries or dependencies to their latest, most stable versions.

6.2 Best Practices for Managing Maintenance

Effective maintenance requires a structured approach to ensure that issues are identified, prioritized, and addressed promptly without disrupting other development activities. Here are some best practices for managing maintenance effectively.

6.2.1 Establish a Ticketing System

A ticketing system, such as Jira or ServiceNow, allows users to report issues, track bug status, and manage support requests. A centralized system also helps prioritize maintenance tasks and provides transparency across the team.

Benefits: Streamlines issue tracking, enables prioritization, and improves communication with users.

Best Practices: Categorize tickets by severity, track resolution time, and update users on progress regularly.

6.2.2 Prioritize Based on Impact and Urgency

Not all issues are created equal. Prioritizing maintenance tasks based on their impact and urgency ensures that critical issues are addressed promptly, while less urgent requests can be scheduled according to available resources.

Best Practices: Use severity levels (e.g., critical, high, medium, low) to categorize tasks, and consider factors such as user impact, security risks, and regulatory requirements.

6.2.3 Perform Regular Code Reviews and Refactoring

Over time, codebases can accumulate "technical debt"—inefficient or outdated code that can increase the risk of issues and slow down future development. Regular code reviews and refactoring help maintain code quality and improve long-term maintainability.

Benefits: Improves performance, reduces the likelihood of bugs, and makes future updates easier.

Best Practices: Schedule code reviews regularly, refactor code to improve readability and efficiency, and document changes to track improvements.

6.2.4 Monitor System Health and Performance

Continuous monitoring allows teams to detect issues before they impact users, enabling proactive maintenance. Monitoring tools like New Relic, Datadog, and Splunk provide real-time insights into system performance, usage patterns, and potential issues.

Benefits: Early detection of performance issues, better resource allocation, and reduced downtime.

Best Practices: Set up alerts for critical metrics, regularly review performance reports, and optimize resources based on usage patterns.

6.2.5 Schedule Routine Maintenance Windows

Routine maintenance windows provide dedicated time to perform updates, apply patches, and optimize performance without affecting users. Scheduling maintenance ensures that regular upkeep activities are not neglected and that the software remains stable and up-to-date.

Best Practices: Communicate maintenance schedules to users, conduct testing in a staging environment, and use automated scripts to streamline updates.

6.3 Managing Updates and Enhancements

Updating software to add new features, improve usability, or optimize performance is an essential part of keeping it relevant. However, managing updates effectively requires a careful balance to avoid disruption while delivering value.

6.3.1 Feature Toggles and Gradual Rollouts

Feature toggles allow teams to enable or disable features in production without redeploying the code. This approach enables gradual rollouts, where features are released to a subset of users first, allowing for controlled testing and feedback.

Benefits: Reduces risk, allows A/B testing, and provides flexibility to modify features post-deployment.

Best Practices: Use feature toggles for non-critical enhancements, monitor user feedback, and enable rollback if issues arise.

6.3.2 Version Control and Documentation

Maintaining version control and thorough documentation helps track changes, manage dependencies, and maintain clarity as the software evolves. Each update should be documented with clear release notes detailing what's new, changed, or fixed.

Best Practices: Use version control systems like Git, document all changes and dependencies, and maintain release notes for transparency with users.

6.3.3 Communicate Updates to Users

Informing users about new updates, changes, and features increases user engagement and provides transparency. Release notes, email notifications, or in-app messages can be used to announce updates.

Benefits: Increases user satisfaction and reduces confusion, especially when significant changes are made.

Best Practices: Use clear, user-friendly language in announcements, highlight new features, and provide support resources for users to learn about updates.

6.4 Handling User Support and Feedback

User support and feedback are integral to effective maintenance. Listening to users provides insights into issues and areas for improvement, while responsive support helps resolve issues quickly and maintains user trust.

6.4.1 Set Up a Feedback Loop

A feedback loop allows users to report issues, suggest improvements, and share their experiences. Channels like in-app feedback forms, user surveys, or dedicated support portals help teams understand how the software performs in real-world usage.

Best Practices: Provide accessible feedback channels, regularly review and analyze feedback, and use insights to inform maintenance and future updates.

6.4.2 Respond Promptly to Support Requests

Timely responses to support requests enhance user satisfaction and demonstrate a commitment to quality. Clear, empathetic communication can turn a frustrated user into a loyal one.

Best Practices: Set response time targets, use ticketing systems to track support requests, and provide users with regular updates on resolution progress.

6.4.3 Gather Data for Continuous Improvement

Analyzing support tickets, feedback, and usage data

allows teams to identify recurring issues, prioritize improvements, and optimize the software based on user needs.

Best Practices: Track and categorize common issues, perform root cause analysis for frequent bugs, and incorporate findings into the maintenance strategy.

6.5 Key Takeaways and Best Practices

The Maintenance and Support phase is essential for keeping software reliable, secure, and aligned with user needs. Here are the key takeaways:

Categorize Maintenance Activities: Use corrective, adaptive, perfective, and preventive maintenance to address issues based on their nature and urgency.

Prioritize Based on Impact: Focus on issues that impact users, security, or compliance first.

Use Monitoring and Ticketing Systems: Monitor system performance and use a ticketing system to track and prioritize maintenance tasks.

Communicate with Users: Keep users informed of updates, maintenance schedules, and support options to enhance their experience.

Incorporate User Feedback: Use user feedback and usage data to identify areas for improvement and guide future updates.

The Maintenance and Support phase ensures that the software remains valuable and functional throughout its lifecycle. With proactive maintenance, user-centered support, and continuous improvement, teams can extend the software's lifespan, reduce downtime, and maintain user satisfaction.

CONCLUSION

The Software Development Lifecycle is a journey that transforms an idea into a reliable, high-quality product. Each phase—Planning, Design, Development, Testing, Deployment, and Maintenance—plays a crucial role in delivering software that meets user needs, adapts to changing environments, and sustains long-term value.

Quality Assurance is integral to every phase, ensuring that the software not only works but excels, meeting the highest standards of functionality, performance, and security. By adopting best practices, leveraging automation, and prioritizing user feedback, development teams can produce software that drives success and satisfaction in

Final Thoughts

Creating exceptional software is not just about

writing code; it's about crafting an experience that resonates with users, meets business goals, and adapts to the constantly evolving technology landscape. Each phase of the Software Development Lifecycle (SDLC) is an opportunity to add value, mitigate risks, and enhance the end product. Quality Assurance (QA) weaves through each phase, ensuring that the final product is not just functional but reliable, secure, and user-friendly.

In this book, we've journeyed through the SDLC, exploring the roles and responsibilities within each phase and uncovering the importance of thorough planning, thoughtful design, rigorous testing, careful deployment, and proactive maintenance. As technology and user expectations continue to evolve, so too will the tools, methodologies, and practices that drive the software industry. But the principles of quality, communication, and continuous improvement remain timeless.

A Commitment to Continuous Improvement

The SDLC is not a static framework; it's a dynamic process that benefits from continuous learning and adaptation. As development teams gain insights from each project, they refine their processes, incorporate new technologies, and enhance their skills. Quality Assurance encourages this iterative growth, advocating for continuous feedback and the pursuit of excellence.

Embracing Collaboration and Communication

The success of software development hinges not only on technical skills but also on effective collaboration and communication across teams. Each phase of the SDLC involves contributions from developers, designers, testers, project managers, and stakeholders. Open, transparent communication helps align goals, prevent misunderstandings, and foster a shared commitment to quality.

Empowering Users and Building Trust

Ultimately, the goal of any software project is to serve its users. Whether the software is intended for individuals, businesses, or entire industries, the end user's experience is paramount. By listening to users, responding to their needs, and maintaining a high standard of quality, software teams build trust and create products that users rely on and appreciate.

Looking Ahead: The Future of Software Development

As we look to the future, technologies like artificial intelligence, machine learning, cloud computing, and DevOps continue to reshape the software landscape. The core principles of the SDLC will remain essential, but they will be augmented by automation, predictive analytics, and increasingly powerful tools. Quality Assurance will evolve alongside these advancements, leveraging new techniques to ensure quality across complex, interconnected systems.

IN CLOSING

Code to Completion: Ensuring Quality Through the Software Development Lifecycle is not just a guide for building software; it's a blueprint for creating lasting value. Whether you're a developer, project manager, tester, or stakeholder, understanding the SDLC and embracing Quality Assurance allows you to contribute meaningfully to successful, user-centered software.

In software development, quality is both a journey and a destination. By integrating quality at every phase, you not only ensure a successful release but also create a foundation for growth, innovation, and user satisfaction. May this book serve as a resource, a reference, and an inspiration as you navigate your own projects from code to completion, always with quality at the heart of your work.